MASTER YOUR EMOTIONS

How to Overcome Negativity, Manage Feelings & End Anxiety

TABLE OF CONTENTS

INTRODUCTION 1

CHAPTER ONE: UNVEILING THE HUMAN EMOTIONS 4

WHAT IS EMOTION? 5

YOUR EMOTION IS A GIFT 7

UNDERSTANDING YOUR EMOTIONAL NEEDS .. 8

THE COMPONENTS OF YOUR EMOTIONS 10

SCIENCE AND YOUR EMOTIONS' FORMATION 14

CHAPTER TWO: THE FORMS OF EMOTION 17

THE SIX BASIC TYPES OF EMOTIONS 18

HAPPINESS 19

SADNESS 21

DISGUST 24

ANGER 25

SURPRISE 27

THE SECONDARY EMOTIONS 28

CHAPTER THREE: DEALING WITH EMOTIONS IN KNOWLEDGE 32

YOUR SEX AND EMOTIONS 33

YOUR CULTURE AND EMOTIONS 35

YOUR EMOTIONS AND MOOD 38

YOUR EMOTIONS AND FEELINGS 40

CHAPTER FOUR: IDENTIFYING AND DEALING WITH EMOTIONAL TRIGGERS....42

YOUR EMOTIONAL TRIGGERS 43

DEALING WITH YOUR EMOTIONAL TRIGGERS

....44

CHAPTER FIVE: THE INFLUENCE OF YOUR EMOTIONS 50

CHAPTER SIX: MASTERING YOUR EMOTIONS 56

INTRODUCTION

Emotions are inherent features of every living human. They are attached to our core beings, values, belief systems, and behavior. The emotions we exhibit are what depict us as creatures filled with feelings d control over what happens around him or her. However, there are many people who have lost control of their emotions. Losing control of your emotions makes you become a ship captain that has lost control of his ship. The ship will tend toward wherever it wishes with a lot of damages guaranteed. Lack of control over a person's emotions will hamper his or her relationship with others, and will also make the person live less than his or her worth. The good news about your emotions is that you have a certain degree of control over them. Your understanding of this reality is what will determine how well you would utilize your control over your emotions.

We live in a world that is full of demands. Your workplace has a lot it demands from you. Coping with the depressing issues of life and the assignment from our work can, at times, lead to anxiety and cause damage to a person's health. When a person feels threatened, he or she will tilt toward placing the blame on his or her challenges on others, which is an action that everyone needs to avoid to live a normal and fulfilling life. You cannot do without facing challenges, and others will always have inputs in your life as you interact with them on a daily basis. The way to put your emotions under control is to understand its intricacies and work toward that.

This book – *Mastering Your Emotions* is a guide that will assist you on how best you can deal with your emotions and make it work out rightly. I have outlined the steps you need to take, and all you need to know to have control over your emotions. In this book, you will learn about the component of emotions, the different kinds of emotions, the factors that trigger your emotion, and how to deal with the triggers, the influence of your emotions on you, and the methods you can take to place your emotions under your control. I expect to see you soon on the first page of this book as you embark on the journey toward mastering your emotions.

CHAPTER ONE: UNVEILING THE HUMAN EMOTIONS

People have a different psychological frame of mind daily. For some, they feel bad, while others feel good. Many people who feel bad do not have an answer to the core root of their feeling of sadness. They often ascribe it to what others have done, or probably their unpalatable personal experiences. It is not uncommon for people to have unwanted emotions that even they do not understand how it came about. It is like you misunderstanding a baby's cry because it needs to change its diapers for hunger. When you offer a baby that is only interested in changing its wet and soaked diaper food, you are merely giving the wrong medication for a specific illness. The truth is that the baby's emotions will not change since you are yet to tend what it needs. Understanding your emotions is a basic skill you need for you to deal with your emotions.

WHAT IS EMOTION?

Emotion is a psychological reality or state that is connected to the nervous system but makes to reflect as a result of chemical changes that are related to thoughts, feelings, responses from behaviors, and a certain level of pleasure or displeasure. Defining human emotions will be unempirical. There is no specific definition that one can give emotion, and this is because emotions have garnered a lot of interest from different fields of studies. It is connected with varying experiences of humans, including mood, temperament, personality, disposition, and motivation. The varying fields that showed interest in emotion include psychology, endocrinology, neuroscience, history, medicine, sociology, and even computer science; hence, its importance.

Human emotion's importance lies in its mental activity, which is an inherent influence over a person. Emotion is an experience, which may be positive or negative that is related to a specific pattern of physiological activity. From your emotions, you begin to experience particular changes, which are behavioral and cognitive. The human emotions are quite complex. As revealed by studies, human emotions are a set of feelings that result in physical and psychological changes that influence our behavior. One important thing you need to note is that your emotions are primarily linked to your behavior, which is an important factor determining how far you would go in all that you do. There is a significant link between emotions and the behavioral tendencies of a person. Extroverts have a high tendency to be social and to express their emotions. However, introverts tend to withdraw from being social, and they often make moves to conceal their emotions. Also, there is a strong belief that emotion drives motivation in a very crucial way. Your emotions as a person is a vital fragment part of your life that you must pay attention to if you must make an indelible mark in all that you do. Despite the studies on emotions and its universality as an element of every human being, emotion is a gift.

YOUR EMOTION IS A GIFT

Your emotion is a gift that you received from the creator. You ought to show gratitude for it. Your emotion is a gift because it is always with you; it is going nowhere. The knowledge that your emotion is going nowhere is part of all you need to have control over your emotions. With your emotions, you make a great difference from robots. Though robots are efficient at what they do, they are non-feeling machines. The robots out there do not know the essence of feelings; however, our emotions reveal what we feel to us. We have access to what goes on around us, and we know it when harm is fast approaching us. Your emotions give you information about what you need to do and how you should act toward certain circumstances. Your emotion is a gift because it makes you know when you need to stand up for yourself and be assertive. It helps you to embrace all that is beneficial to you and dissociate from what does not benefit you.

Understanding your emotions will empower you more to utilize your emotions as a gift. You will understand how much you need to care for yourself, and most importantly, for others. Emotions help to make the right decisions from the inner hints, without relying on external advisers. It helps us to form relationships that are beneficial to us and others and points to our basic needs, which once they are met, we will experience a significant sense of fulfillment. Hence, you should avoid dismissing your emotions while you start paying attention to it.

UNDERSTANDING YOUR EMOTIONAL NEEDS

Your emotions have needs. The earlier you understand this, the better it is for you. Understanding what your emotional needs are will help you to utilize it appropriately to have good control over your life. Emotional needs are specific and particular to each person. Also, the emotional needs of a person are usually formed from childhood. Your environment and the people that surround you will determine the needs that your emotions will require. This is one reason every individual has distinct emotional needs. A practical example is a child whose parents did not give much attention while growing up; however, the sibling was mainly attended to. Such a child will grow up certain craving needs, which includes the need to be appreciated and recognized. When such a person does not see it, he or she will experience a bad emotional experience. For the beloved sibling, he or she would have grown with the mindset of always being the center of attention in every place he or she meets himself; this is because that is what he or she has lived with over the years.

When a child grows up, he or she will be interested in satisfying his or her emotional needs. The inability of the child to provide emotional needs often leads to emotional pains. The child who needs appreciation form others would experience emotional pains if he or she does not get it from others. Usually, when such a person feels emotional pains, he or she is oblivious to the reason behind the feeling. The truth is, you cannot live a fulfilled life if you do not know your emotional needs. The knowledge of your emotional needs is crucial for you to know how you can deal with every pain you experience. One of the commonest emotional pain is *Depression.* The mind uses the pain that a person feels as a motivation to pursue the person's unfulfilled emotional needs. The feeling of depression and sadness is what a person comes up with when he or she is not getting what he or she desires emotionally. Though these are pains to a person's emotion, however, they are the motivations that the mind could come up with to deal head-on with a person's needs. The understanding of your emotional needs will help you to identify the causes of your emotional pains.

THE COMPONENTS OF YOUR EMOTIONS

There are five components of human emotions. These components are the basic ingredients and building blocks that direct the workings of our emotions. A person's experience of motion is coordinated and synchronized for a short period of time by all of these components. The components are arranged in a processing model. The processing model gives the sequence of events that describe the coordination that is involved during an emotional experience. The components are:

Cognitive Appraisal: *It* gives a detailed evaluation of activities and objects. There have, however, been disparities in the relationship that exists between emotions and cognitive appraisal. Cognitive appraisal is based on the subjective interpretation an individual give to stimuli in an environment. It relates to emotions, as well as stress, coping, and mental health. Cognitive appraisal details how a person reacts or responds to life stressors. The cognitive component helps to analyze how an individual picks up on a situation, action, individuals, or environment that has an influence on the emotion. It will aid an individual in understanding how these stimuli impact his or her life. At the same time, the person will find it easy to communicate the state of his or her internal world to others.

Bodily Symptoms: This comprises of the physiological components of a person's emotional experience. It gives support to other components, and it is the chemical reaction that a person's body experiences. For instance, when a person is angry, there will be a rush of blood flowing to the hands.

Tendencies for Action: This component is involved in the preparation and direction of a person's motor responses. When an emotion is identified, the body will move into a particular action. Human emotions bestow specific actions rather than others. This explains why some actions are beyond our control, while others are not.

Expressive Component: This component involves the accompaniment of facial and vocal expressions with the emotional state to relate reactions and intention of actions. It reflects how a person communicates his or her experiences through the use of facial expressions, body movements, gestures, etc.

Feeling Component: It is the personal experience of an emotional state immediately it occurs. It is the component that shows the state of the feeling in an individual. It involves monitoring the internal universe and the recognition of what the person is experiencing at a point in time.

Everyone has the components of emotions; however, the intensity and our expression of emotions are quite different. There are certain social factors (I will discuss these factors in a later chapter) that affect and breed these differences in us. Let me go practical with you. For example, when you hear statements like "I am really afraid," "I am feeling jittery," "I do not want to visit this place" or "I do not have enough time to prepare for the final," these are all parts of the forms of emotions components. Starting with the first statement, "I am really afraid," this describes a personal feeling of fear. The second statement, "I am feeling jittery," it depicts a physiological component of emotion. While the third statement, "I don't want to visit this place," shows an avoidance action tendency. The fourth statement "I do not have enough time to prepare for the final" is used to describe several appraisals of the events, which may be interpreted to mean the following; a frustration (I am not prepared for it), or lack of power (I do not have enough time). Motor activities that are connected to emotions include facial expressions such as frowning, smiling, body posture, etc. (you will learn about this in a later chapter)

SCIENCE AND YOUR EMOTIONS' FORMATION

If you want to have control over your emotions, the knowledge of how it is formed is quite important. The formation of a person's emotions is largely connected to the activities that happen in the brain. Neuroscience gives a detailed explanation of it. According to discoveries through the neural mapping of the limbic system, a neurobiological explanation to human emotions was given. The discovery claimed that emotion is a pleasant or an unpleasant mental state that is organized in the limbic system of the mammalian brain. Emotions, when it is distinguished from the reactive responses of reptiles, is an elaboration of general vertebrate arousal patterns. It involves the activities of neurochemicals, such as dopamine, noradrenaline, and serotonin that step up or step down the level of the brain's activity, as reflected physically in body movements, postures, and gestures. Also, it is possible for pheromones to mediate in the activities of emotions. A good example is the emotion of love. It is said to be the expression of Paleocircuits of the mammalian brain, which helps in the facilitation of the care, feeding, and grooming of infants. Paleocircuits are neural platforms that work for body expression configuration before the cortical circuits for speech are activated.

Emotions relate to specific activities that go on in the brain areas that specifically direct our attention, give our behavior motivations, and portray the importance of what happens around us. Earlier studies revealed that emotion is linked with a group of structures at the center of the human brain called the limbic system. The limbic system includes the hypothalamus, cingulate cortex, hippocampi, and many other structures. Some of these limbic structures are directly related to emotions, while some are not. In addition, the prefrontal cortex has been linked with emotion. There were two neurological models of emotions in the prefrontal cortex that made opposing predictions. According to the Valence Model, anger, which is a negative emotion would activate the right prefrontal cortex, while The Direction Model predicted that anger, which is an approach emotion would activate the left prefrontal cortex. The second model was, however, accepted. Nonetheless, the two models depict that the activities of your emotion can be traced to the brain. Hence there is a connection between the human brain and his or her emotion.

CHAPTER TWO:
THE FORMS OF EMOTION

There have been studies on the different types of emotions that exist. Many forms of emotions truly have an influence on how we live our lives and our interaction with others. At times, a person is ruled by these emotions (which should not be). Our emotions at every point in time has a level of influence on our choices, our actions, and our perceptions about things and people around us; however, they should never control any of these. There have been moves by psychologists to identify the forms of emotions that we experience. As a result, some theories emerged to give us a categorization of the kinds of emotions that we experience. One such Psychologist who made efforts was Paul Eckman.

Paul Eckman identified six basic types of emotions that every human experience, regardless of our culture. The six basic emotions are; Happiness, Sadness, Disgust, Fear, Surprise, and Anger. Aside from these basic types, there are other secondary forms, such as Pride, Shame, Embarrassment, and excitement. The understanding of these basic types is a good move toward having control over your emotions. You need to identify a problem if you must solve it.

THE SIX BASIC TYPES OF EMOTIONS

The basic emotions are often combined in our daily experiences. They can be combined with other basic emotions or secondary emotions to form a new feeling. When we combine emotions, we achieve different feelings, just like the mixing of colors to form different shades. The combination of basic emotions acts like building blocks for specific feelings.

An example is the mixing of the primary emotion of Happiness and Trust to arrive at Love. Nonetheless, each of these basic forms of emotions has an impact on our experiences. Let's go through them and consider their impacts on us all.

HAPPINESS

Happiness is the most sought-after emotion among the basic six. We all want to be happy. When we were in school, there is the feeling of "I want to win the best prize for Arithmetic in my class so I can make my mom and dad proud." We all enjoy it when we receive a promotion, or probably a new contract just clicked. Happiness is a pleasant emotional state with unique characteristics, such as contentment, gratifications, joy, satisfaction, and well-being. Aside from our general interest in Happiness, even the field of positive psychology had shown interest in it. Happiness is expressed. Usually, a person gets to express his or her of happiness through facial expressions, such as smiling. It could also be expressed through body language, such as having a relaxed stance. Also, it is often depicted through the tone of voice of a person, which will be pleasant.

Generally, while we believe that Happiness is the most important of all human emotions, we do not have a full understanding that Happiness tends to rely greatly on the influence of our culture. There are conventional acts that most people follow nowadays, even parents. You will hear them tell their children to go to school, have good grades, and become a graduate so the child can become something great in the future. The result of the advice lies in the child having a happy life. However, when you are faced with realities, you would discover that what contributes to Happiness is much more complex, and individualized than the conventional beliefs and orientation. The connection that has been created between wealth and Happiness by people has been existing for decades. Well, to some extent, there is Happiness in wealth. However, that is not in every case. We have cases of wealthy persons who are not in good condition. They have challenges with their health and, as such, cannot claim they are happy.

Moreover, Happiness itself is linked with both the psychological and Physiological health of a person. Studies have mentioned that Happiness has a relationship with various consequences such as increased marital satisfaction and longevity, while a lack of Happiness at the same time has been linked to various poor health conditions. When there is a lack of Happiness, the following will surface anxiety, depression, stress, and loneliness, and these lead to a decrease in immunity, an increase in inflammation, and a decrease in life expectancy.

SADNESS

Unlike Happiness, Sadness is a transient emotional state. It has specific features such as grief, disappointment, hopelessness, disinterest, and dampened the mood. Just like every other emotion, people often experience sadness. However, we all despise it. Sadness can be prolonged and severe in certain circumstances. In such cases, Sadness will become depression. Just like Happiness, Sadness is also expressed through the following manners: quietness, dampened mood, withdrawal from other people, Lethargy, and crying. The severity of Sadness is determined by the cause and the reaction of a person to it. We all react and cope with Sadness differently. For some people, when they are sad, they tend to adopt different coping mechanisms, such as avoiding people, ruminating on negative thoughts, and self-medicating.   These actions are injurious to a person's health, and they breed Sadness to have a longer duration than it is supposed to have, plays a major role in the survival of an individual. It is a powerful emotion. Fear as emotion often occurs as the fight or flight response. We experience fear as a response to danger. When a person experiences fear, the muscles tend to become tense, there will be an increase in the heartbeat and respiration of a person, and the mind will become more alert. All these activities will send information to your body, which is to either run from the danger or wait to fight it head-on. With the response a person gets from fear, he or she will be prepared to make the decision on how to deal with threats in his or her environment. There are other expressions of fear, which include facial expression, such as the widening of eyes and pulling back of the chin, attempting to hide or flee from the threat, or probably physical reaction, such as rapid breathing.

We do not all have the same experience with fear. The rate of our sensitivity to fear differs, and the triggers also differ. Some objects are likely to make someone afraid, while another person will be less afraid of them. The specific situations may trigger fear in a person when it does not call for an alarm for others. What fear does primarily is to make us respond to whatever we consider a threat. We do not have to see the threat before we react. A person may react to an anticipated threat, or a potential danger, which is what we call anxiety. The anxiety can come in the form of social anxiety, which is the fear of social situations. While some people are afraid of specific events such as extreme sports, and another thrill that is fear-inducing, others take solace in them and find them amusing; hence, the source of fear for everyone differs. Also, when a person becomes used to a scary object or situation, familiarity will be built and acclimation. These will reduce the feelings of fear and anxiety in such a person. This knowledge births the *Exposure*

Therapy, which exposes people to what frightens them in a controlled and safe manner. With this, there will be a reduction in the feeling of fear.

DISGUST

Disgust is one of the basic emotions common to everyone. It is often displayed in different ways, including moving away from the object that disgusts, through physical reactions such as vomiting, or retching, and through facial expression such as curling the upper lip and wrinkling the nose. Disgust involves a sense of revulsion, which often originates from several situations and objects such as an unpleasant taste, smell, or sight. Many studies have claimed that the emotion of Disgust evolved as a reaction to foods that were likely to be harmful. The smell or taste of foods that have gone bad often birth this reaction. The triggers of Disgust include poor hygiene, blood, rot, infection, and death. It can be the body's method of avoiding whatever has the propensity to transmit disease. Disgust can be against immoral behaviors. If you find others doing what is outside your belief, and acceptable acts, you may find them distasteful, immoral, or evil.

ANGER

Anger is a powerful emotion we all feel. In some cultures, it is quite believed that a person needs to get angry in certain situations. This is actually in opposition to what many people believe. We all want to stay away from anger. The world has a picture of the destructive end of anger, how it negatively impacts us, and our relationships with others. The emotion of Anger comes with agitation, hostility, frustration, and usually, antagonism toward the other person. Anger can also be used as a fight or flight response against fear. Danger or threat can generate Anger in a person, which the person will resort to as a means of combatting the danger and protecting himself or herself. Anger is displayed through facial expressions such as frowning or glaring, body language, which include taking a strong stance or moving away from the person you are angry at. The tone of voice of a person can also depict Anger, such as yelling or speaking gruffly. The physiological responses can be sweating, or the person's eyes are turning red. It may also be hitting, kicking, or throwing of objects, which is what we are all familiar with.

However, in opposition to the general claim that Anger is bad, Anger can be good at times. You only need to be mindful of it. When it is constructive, it will help a person to make certain clarifications in his or her relationships. It may also be of help to you by motivating you to take action and identify solutions to whatever it is that is bothering you. Anger becomes negative when it is expressed excessively or in an unhealthy manner. You need to place your anger under control so that it will not become aggression, which can lead to harming others, and violence.

Anger can breed both Psychological and Physical consequences. When you lose control of your anger, it will be difficult to make the right decisions. More than the havoc that may happen to the other party, Anger can also impact you negatively. It has been linked to coronary heart diseases and diabetes. It also influences certain health risks, such as alcohol consumption, aggressive driving, and smoking.

SURPRISE

The surprise is the sixth basic type of emotion identified by Eckman. The surprise does not stay for long, and it is followed by a physiological response of startling, which often occurs as a result of an unexpected event. Surprise an either be positive, negative or even neutral depending on the event that necessitates it. For instance, imagine a person jumping out from behind a tree as you walk to your car at night, there will be an unpleasant surprise in such a scenario.

On the other hand, if you get home and find your family members, including those living far away waiting to celebrate your birthday with you, you would perhaps have a pleasant surprise. The surprise is characterized by facial expressions, including raising of your brows, opening your mouth, and widening of the eyes. There are also physical and verbal reactions, such as jumping back and screaming, yelling, or gasping, respectively.

Moreover, Surprise serves as a trigger of fight or flight response. When you are startled, your adrenaline can increase and helps you prepare your body to either stay to fight to flee. Surprise affects a person's behavior. According to studies, people tend to notice surprising events in a disproportionate manner. This is the reason surprising and unusual events in the news often stand out in people's memory than other events. We often learn more from surprising information, and we easily get swayed by surprising arguments.

THE SECONDARY EMOTIONS

The basic emotions are just a few of the different forms of emotions that we can experience. One thing about these basic emotions is that they are universal, and experienced by everyone regardless of the culture. One other thing that is common to the basic emotions is their expression through the face. However, some of the secondary emotions I will be identifying here are not expressed through facial expression. Also, it is safe to say that these secondary emotions are sometimes the result of the basic emotions. When a person experiences the basic emotions, there is a tendency that he or she will react in a specific way, which may be another emotion. Below are some of the possible secondary emotions:

Contentment: It can happen as a result of Happiness. Happiness is what we all want, and once we experience it, there will be an emotional reality of contentment in us.

Contempt: Content can arise as a result of uncontrolled anger, which often leads to aggression. Also, when something triggers disgust emotions, it can build up the emotion of contempt from a person toward the disgusting object or act.

Embarrassment: The feeling of embarrassment can come following a surprising phenomenon. Imagine you being asked a question you do not have an answer to in public, or probably, you are engaging in an argument, and the opponent gives a strong point you cannot counter. Your reaction at the point may be that embarrassment.

Relief: We all fill relieved once we set goals, and they are accomplished. Also, after encountering certain surprising event, which ends up being pleasant, there can be a sense of relief in the heart of a person.

Pride in achievement: This is related to contentment. When a person sets and achieves his or her goals, there is a possibility of feeling proud about it. Pride can be positive or negative in this case. It will serve positively if it empowers the person by motivating him or her to do more; however, if it makes the person see whatever he or she has done as the best anyone could do, it becomes negative.

Guilt: The emotion of guilt needs to be dealt with. It can result from the events that precede an uncontrolled Anger expression. When Anger is not channeled rightly, it may lead to harmful results that a person may end up experience.

Shame: This can come as a result of a surprising event, just like embarrassment. Also, an unchecked Anger can birth it too. Shame has never embraced in any culture. We all want to run away from it. More reason it is essential for you to have control over your emotions in order to avoid specific demeaning results such as shame.

Emotions do not occur in isolation. There are gradients of emotions, and the different emotions are related. A better clarification of the nature of your emotion will aid you in understanding the way you behave in certain situations, your mood, and a means of living a better life that is devoid of uncontrollable emotions. The crucial role of emotions in our lives cannot be overemphasized. It ranges from influencing our interactions with others daily to the decisions we make. None of your emotion is an island, and many of the emotions that we experience are nuanced and complex. They work together to create the rich and distinct fabric of our emotional life.

CHAPTER THREE: DEALING WITH EMOTIONS IN KNOWLEDGE

I have unveiled the intricacies of emotions to you, and at the same time, you have come to the realization of the different forms of emotion that a person can experience. In this chapter, I will further explain some specific factors that are closely related to our emotions. Many people do not understand the differences and relationships that exist between their emotions and this factor. Your understanding of the relationship will serve as a building block toward gaining control over your emotions without the lack of knowledge of how any of them operate. Many people who lack control over their emotions find themselves in such a situation as a consequence of their ignorance about some of these factors. The best way to keep your emotions under control is to have knowledge about what it is and what it is not. Below, I will be taking you through how your emotions relate to gender, culture, your facial expression, mood, and feelings.

YOUR SEX AND EMOTIONS

There have been different arguments on the kind of relationship that exists between gender and emotions. The question asked borders on if there is a difference in the manner, which men and women express their emotions. Generally, there is a Stereotype view that women are more emotional than men. Based on this, to be more specific, there is the belief that women experience and express discrete emotions such as fear, disgust, happiness, and sadness more than men do. Nonetheless, there is the general acceptance by different researchers that the differences in the expression of emotions by men and women originate from the socialization of the roles of gender, rather than biological. As a result, the emotional expression experienced by a specific population is often based on their cultural expectations for the female and male gender.

Moreover, the views of Psychologists on sex and emotions differ. Many of them reject the notion that women are more emotional than men. Instead, they opined that men are only restrictive in their expression of emotions. This is called *Restrictive Emotionality*, which is a tendency to inhibit the expression of a specific emotion. It is an unwillingness to reveal intimate feelings by oneself. This act by men has an influence on their health, emotional appraisal, and their overall identity. Also, it tends to increase the risk of certain anxiety disorders in them. Based on researches, women show less restrictive tendencies toward their emotions than men because it is what they grow up with. At a very tender age of 4 to 6, the girl child tends to express more sadness and anxiety than her male counterpart. Also, the female always smiles, and laughs, and nods more the male, while the male child from childhood has the tendency to be angry. The expressive nature of women is across cultures.

Women also tend to express their emotions, such as anger in solitary, while men do not care less about their appearing positive to others; hence, they feel free to express their emotions without restraint. The general area of connection between gender and emotion is that women tend to express their emotions more than the male counterpart. However, there is a plausible explanation for it all. The expression of emotions by both men and women is susceptible to certain social factors. There are specific social and cultural standards that may reinforce the differences in the expression of emotions by men and women.

YOUR CULTURE AND EMOTIONS

The relationship that exists between your culture and emotions lies in the structure, guidelines, expectations, and rules that our culture provides us. All these help us to interpret, understand, and express our emotions. For every culture, there is a specific standard that rules the frequencies of an individual emotional display, which is considered acceptable by a given culture. How positive and negative emotions are to be expressed is contained in the *Cultural Scripts* of every culture. The script serves as the body that regulates how people within the confines of a specific culture should conduct their emotions, which is a form of influence on our emotional experience. Culture is a shared set of beliefs, norms, values, attitudes, and behavior that is centralized around a specific theme and specific to a group of people who speak the same language.

Furthermore, our cultural background and context determine our reactions to a different mode of communication. Our culture tends to act as cues when we try to interpret the facial expressions of others. As a result, different cultures have the tendencies to interpret the same facial expression in different ways. Regardless of the differences in the rules that guide our emotional expressions, there is a universality in our ability to recognize and produce basic facial expressions of emotions. The basic emotions are expressed by all, regardless of our cultures and background. However, other complex emotions, including jealousy, love, and pride, are dependent on cultural influences than the basic emotions.

A practical example of the influence of culture on emotion's expression is the Asian culture. In Asia, they prioritize social harmony over personal gain, however, in the United States, there is the prioritization of self-promotion, and this is obtainable in most European States. From studies, it was revealed that individuals from the US are more likely to express their emotions both positive and negative while they are alone or in public; however, an Asian, such a Japanese will most likely express his or her emotions while alone. Also, people who are from cultures that lay emphasis on social cohesion are most likely going to suppress their emotional expression while they first evaluate the best response for a specific situation. The consequences attached to the expression of emotions in different cultures differ. In the US, for example, a man will be ostracized both directly and indirectly for crying in public. Daily, we are fed with the information on what facial expression is. And we tend to be bound by the requirements of our cultures in our expression of emotions.

YOUR EMOTIONS AND MOOD

When mention is made of emotions, some people tend to confuse it with mood. However, they are different. When you understand what mood is, and emotion is, you will gain understanding more about yourself, and get to know others better. The mood is emotional feelings. It often lasts longer than emotions; it can last up to one or two days. When a person moves into his or her mood closets, it often seems like stages that he or she is going through, and it is quite difficult to shift. Moods are often results of particular circumstances such as pressure at home, and work, financial challenges, etc. and as long as these circumstances are still there, a person tends to maintain the same mood.

On the other hand, emotions come and go as quickly as possible. They may be positive or negative, and they may be caused by specific circumstantial factors, such as what someone does or says. Emotions are often sharper than moods, and they vary. A person can express different emotions, but the mood is often generalized, it can either be a bad or a good mood. A little occurrence or object may trigger and change a person's emotions faster. When a person experiences emotions and mood at the same time, the emotions will stay in the mood. It is possible for a person who is in a bad mood to have a brief period of happiness and joy. Also, when a person is in a good mood, it is possible for him or her to feel sad or angry briefly.

Nonetheless, our emotions may have a similar flavor to our mood. That is, our emotions are susceptible to the mood we find ourselves in, and this affects how we interpret our environment in specific ways. When a person is in a bad mood, it is quite possible for him or her to interpret things in light of the bad mood. When you understand your mood and emotions, you would see that at times, when you feel angry and frustrated, the feeling is not caused by those around you, but by a mood have been nursing, and others should not be blamed for that.

YOUR EMOTIONS AND FEELINGS

It is also important to understand the difference between emotions and feelings. The knowledge can help you to change your unhealthy behaviors and embrace peace and happiness. Though feelings and emotions are interconnected, they are different. Emotions are responses at the lower level in the subcortical regions of the brain, which is the amygdala and the ventromedial prefrontal cortices. They create biochemical reactions in a person's body, thereby altering the person's physical state. Though emotional reactions do vary slightly in individuals, depending on the circumstances that birth it, they also are similar universally among all people. An example is smiling that only humans exhibit. Emotional memories can last longer because of the activities of the amygdala that regulates the release of the neurotransmitters that are important for memory consolidation. Emotions often come before feelings; they are physical, and they are instinctual. You can easily measure them through blood flow, facial micro-expressions, and through body language.

Feeling, on the other hand, emanates from the neocortical regions of the brain. Your feelings are mental associations and reactions to your emotions, and they are personal because they are influenced by your experience, memories, and beliefs. Feelings are the psychological portrayal of the happenings in your body when you experience an emotion. It is often the result of your activity working to ascribe a meaning to your emotion. It comes immediately after emotions, and it involves cognitive input, it is usually subconscious, and you cannot measure it precisely. While emotions play out in the theater of our body, feelings play out in the theater of our minds

The emotions and feelings of a person are crucial in his or her experience and interactions with the world. They serve as the driving force working behind many behaviors. Understanding your emotions and feelings will help you to navigate the world and experience it better. A change in your thinking and behavior toward what is wrong around you will help you maintain balance, peace, purpose, and hope toward moving closer to your goals.

CHAPTER FOUR: IDENTIFYING AND DEALING WITH EMOTIONAL TRIGGERS

Usually, when you react badly to an event, there is the tendency that you would want to blame the event for your expression. When your child refuses to do what you requested him or her to do and you had a big-time outburst, you are likely to blame the child for the cause of your reaction also. However, not everyone reacts in the same way. There are people who will rather accept the same acts you reject. For everything you engage yourself in, there is a specific belief, values, or views that you hold. Emotional triggers often work through a person's belief system. Your beliefs determine whether emotional triggers will influence your behaviors or not. At times, emotional triggers can breed good behaviors. However, they breed more negative behaviors. You need to be aware of your emotional triggers so that you can easily gain control over them, and understand the right time for you to intervene between events and your reactions to them so that you can create a desirable situation.

YOUR EMOTIONAL TRIGGERS

A trigger is an experience that draws a person back into the past, and it elicits certain behaviors to arise. Emotional triggers are certain situations or events that may give rise to your emotional expressional expression. There are lots of factors that can trigger a person's emotions. However, below are common ones.

- Requests that do not conform to your belief
- Subjection under a higher authority
- The control of your time by someone else
- Inability to say No, and lack of self-confidence
- When you are being abandoned
- When you are ignored
- When you are criticized
- When you are blamed
- Competitive situation

- Lack of trust in a person, or a person lack of trust in you

Emotional triggers are the super-reactive places inside a person that are activated by another person's behavior or statement. When you are triggered, you may feel hurt or explode with anger as a response. These triggers differ, and they require specific approaches to deal with them. You need to observe your feelings and emotions to identify the specific triggers of your emotions that are giving you an unwanted result.

DEALING WITH YOUR EMOTIONAL TRIGGERS

Identify the External Stimuli

Some of your emotional triggers are social and situational. To deal with your emotional triggers, you have to take note of the situations that make you behave in an unwanted manner. While you do that, you need to take a step further by identifying those who were involved, and the event that happened at the time. By doing this, you will have access to specific patterns that will make it easy for you to deal with your emotional outbursts from its root. Your first goal is to identify and understand the source of your emotional triggers. When you have this knowledge, it will become easier for you to control yourself so you will not be subjected to the triggers in the future. Most times, when people discover that their triggers are external factors, they tend to take a posture of powerlessness. You shouldn't try to think that way. Either it is external or internal, you can always take charge. To deal with external stimuli, you need to adapt yourself to the situation so that the trigger will become familiar and will be inactive to get you emotional. Also, adapt your thinking and behavior o reduce the emotional response you give to the situation. And finally, you should be ready to remove yourself from the situation.

Identify the Internal Triggers

When you discover that your emotion is working in the wrong direction, you need to look inwardly also. Look into your thoughts and your feelings. Your thoughts about people and situations have a significant influence on your behavior. You need to look out for these thoughts because there are times these thoughts are not accurate. When you become aware of your thoughts, it will become easier for you to challenge them. Take all the time; you need to understand your thoughts and feelings. When you have an understanding of a specific emotional trigger, you would know how to identify the need for changes you must make at every point in time when you are being triggered. The internal triggers are reflected in the power of your thought. Always remember that you are what and who you think you are. Your emotional triggers will cause you to think in a specific way, and you begin to believe it, and think of yourself in the same vein. What you think about yourself from the inside has a great influence on how you would behave and be perceived.

Utilize the Help of a Journal

This method involves you keep a good track record of your behavior. You should have a journal that you can use to keep track of how you behave. The records you keep will notify you once you move into unwanted behavior. Always make a record of your thoughts, emotions, and how you feel. While you document this, do not forget to add the situations that incited those feelings in you. Try to be as detailed as possible. Note every single detail of what is happening around you, including what goes on in your head. When you track your triggers, you will have a trace of their roots, and pinpoint the needed steps to deal with them. Also, you will get to know yourself better, which is a hallmark of taking charge of your emotions. However, the understanding of your emotion's trigger roots, and yourself doesn't occur by default. You need to make conscious efforts to see a positive result. Be proactive at identifying what exactly it is that triggers your emotions. You should have this in mind that in the course of keeping your journal, you need to avoid editing. Instead, make sure you write from a stream of consciousness. Editing may leave out an important emotional trigger or information about your triggers.

Learn to Challenge Yourself

One best way to deal with your triggers is to place yourself in a demanding and hard position. At the same time, be opened to doing something new and be more constructive. One easiest way to defeat yourself is to avoid your challenge. Avoidance has never been the key to effectiveness when it comes to facing challenges. It is not effective in solving any problem. You have got to challenge yourself if you must change what you do not like, or deal with your emotional triggers. It has not been easy, and it will not still be easy. However, the eventual rewards justify the means. The earlier you come to the realization that no one will help you solve your triggers problem, the better it is for you. Especially when others are offended by your emotional expressions; they are most likely no going to be of help to you. Rather than move closer, they would rather move away from you. The knowledge you have about what needs to be fixed in your life should propel you to take the necessary steps to fix what requires fixing. You need to challenge yourself to be your best and overcome your emotional triggers. You may be caught in the web of excuse claiming that change is a difficult experience. The reality is that you are aware of what you need to change, and you know that there is a difficulty in your situation already. Deal with that difficulty.

Create Alternatives

To stop your behavior, you need to do more than stop behaving the way you have been behaving. The method is scarcely effective. There is a need for substitution. You should change bad behavior by taking up a good one. For every reaction you express as a result of your emotional triggers, you should identify a better reaction that will suit the situation. Creating an alternative requires you to develop new skills and implement them. Imagine if your trigger is a person who loves making you get angry. If you have been giving in by exploding each time he triggers you, you will not stop yelling at him by stopping to yell. Instead, you would fare better if you could walk out of the building the next time he tries to trigger you. Your alternative should be constructive and rewarding in helping you to control your emotions adequately.

CHAPTER FIVE: THE INFLUENCE OF YOUR EMOTIONS

Emotions influence us and what we do. They play essential roles in our pattern of thinking and behavior. We can hardly separate a person's emotions with his or her daily commitments and activities. We make most of our decisions based on our emotions. The understanding of how your emotions influence you will go a long way in helping you identify how well you are exploring your emotions. You would understand better whether you are expressing your emotions in the right manner or in the wrong direction. There are three aspects you need to be familiar with if you must understand how your emotions influence you.

- The way you experience your emotion – the subjective aspect
- The way your body reacts and expresses the emotions – the physiological aspect

- The manner you behave as a response to your emotion – the expressive aspect

These aspects play crucial roles in the purpose and function of a person's responses. As mentioned earlier, emotions are usually short-lived. It may come in the form of a quick annoyance toward a colleague at work. The question is, what the importance of emotions to a person is? Why do we experience the emotions that we experience? What role do emotions play in our lives?

Emotions Motivate for Action

One important role of emotion for everyone is its ability to propel and motivate us to take action. There are times we feel like doing nothing. However, the emotional experience attached to what we have to do will be the calling bell that will get us ready for the work. For example, when a person is faced with a demanding examination, there will be a mighty wind of anxiety on his or her heart. The anxiety usually surrounds the forecasting of the result of the exam; you want to know what you would have at the end of the day. In such a situation, the emotional response of anxiety will most likely get you up from your bed and place you in a reading mode. The reading mode is to make you achieve what you are anxious about. Also, you may be motivated to take certain steps as a response to the need to experience positive emotions. The motivating role of emotions will make you seek out activities that will make you happy, feel contented, and excited. While you would avoid any situations or activities that might pose any potential danger to you.

Emotions Show us the Way of Survival

As opined by a Naturalist – Charles Darwin, emotions are adaptations that give room for both humans and animals to survive and reproduce. Emotion enables us to confront the source of our irritation whenever we are angry. Through the emotion of fear, one can easily run away from what can take his or her life. Also, when the emotions of love reign supreme, there is the willingness to seek out a mate and start reproducing. Through emotions, we take steps that will maximize our chances of survival and success.

Emotions Help with Decisions making

Our emotions partly determine our decisions. Starting from our decisions in the early part of our day, until late in the night, the influence of our emotions on what decisions we make cannot be overemphasized. Your emotions are at play when you make the decision on what to eat, and the best candidate to vote for in a coming election. According to studies, it has been revealed that people who have brain damage that affects their capacity to experience emotions also experience a decrease in their ability to make good decisions. No matter the decisions, even when logic and rationality are involved, our emotions come to play. When you have a great emotional intelligence prowess, it will become easy for you to make good and sound decisions.

Emotions Help Others to Understand Us

Our interactions with people often involve clues that help them understand our feelings and decisions. The cues we give may involve emotional expression through body language, including different facial expressions that are connected with a particular emotion that we are experiencing. At times, we may have to state categorically and directly our feelings. When you tell people around about your happiness, sadness, or fear, you are giving them information about you that they can utilize to connect with you.

Emotions Give Us Knowledge about Others

Emotions do not just tell others about us. They also give us information about the other person that we see and interact with daily. When people around us express themselves, we receive a wealth of information about them. We are subjected to the need for social communication. It is how we live with others and build our relationships. We need to learn the techniques for interpreting and reacting appropriately to the emotions of others. When we have a deep knowledge of others' emotions, it will become easier to respond to their elicitations, and build a strong and deeper relationship with them. The knowledge also helps to communicate effectively with people in varying social situations. You will be able to deal with customers who seem to be irate or any hot-headed employee. The understanding of the emotional expression of others will give us clear information on how we should respond and relate with them in every situation.

Emotions serve varying purposes. Human emotions can be persistent, fleeting, powerful, complex, and even be life changing. We need to understand its influence in our lives to utilize it effectively for success. They can motivate a person to act in a specific way and provide us the tools that we need to make meaningful interactions possible in our world.

CHAPTER SIX: MASTERING YOUR EMOTIONS

Inherently, nothing is wrong with any form of emotion. However, the loss of control over them is what portrays the wrong aspect of our emotions. Just like every good thing that life has to offer, emotions have their bad sides. No one will ever dispute the importance of water; however, when it is not taken with balance and proper check, it can make one uncomfortable. So also, emotions can lead to a lot of unhealthy realities when a person does not properly check them. It can breed distress, hatred, violence, aggression, and many more when it is left unattended to by a person. These necessitate the need to have a good grasp of our emotions. The hallmark of a complete person is his or her capacity to take charge of his or her emotions against every external factor and internal factors all the same. Your ability to master your emotions is called emotional intelligence. It is a tactful skill that empowers you to understand your emotions and that of others. Your ability to master your emotions has many benefits, such as the following, the ability to cope, improvement in well-being, resilience, and relationship satisfaction. To adequately control your mind, I have six methods you can follow.

#Method 1 – Repositioning Your Mind and Body

The first step to mastering your emotions is to identify when they are moving out of your reach. Our emotions don't fly out at the inception. They crawl out like a snail from its shell. At that point, when you started nursing a swelling in your thoughts or reaction, you need to immediately identify the movement of your emotions so you can easily call it back to order. The ability to identify your emotions when they are being swayed requires mindfulness and conscious and rational thoughts. There are usually tips that you get to know when your emotions are getting out of control. Some of the feelings include:

- Physical reactions, such as an increase in the rate of your heartbeat. Rapid or shallow breathing or tense muscles.

- Psychological reactions may include loss of focus, the feeling of anxiety, or panic, the feeling of overwhelming, or losing control of your thoughts.

At the point in time, when you feel all these, you need to take immediate steps to help you deal with your emotions. To reposition your mind and body at this stage requires you to refocus your attention from the trigger that calls for an increase in your body reactions. You need to take the following steps to reposition your mind and body.

1. Work on your breathing techniques to calm yourself. Once you notice your emotions are getting out of your control, then your breathing will also be drifting away from you as well, and this often compounds a person's anxiety and stress at the same time. Trying the right breathing techniques will help to salvage it. To try this, do the following:

Place one hand on your chest, the other hand below your rib cage. Begin to inhale slowly and deeply through your nose at the count of four. Experience your lungs and abdomen expand as fill them with air. Hold the breath for up to one or two seconds and start to release your breath gradually through your mouth. You can aim further for up to six to ten deep breaths per minute.

2. Place your attention on physical sensations to re-center your mind. When you lose control of your emotions, you are likely to lose yourself and place. You may even lose awareness of yourself. You may give yourself to grounding exercises. It will root you in the present moment and stops your emotional spiral.

3. You should learn to relax your muscles to relieve your physical and mental tensions. You need to look into yourself and identify the part of your body where the stress is being held. Relax the area to let go of the stress. You can do this by unclenching your hands, relaxing your shoulders, and allow the stress to leave through legs. You can also roll your neck and shake out your fingers.

4. You can utilize visualization to calm yourself in a calm or safe place. Get yourself a place that you can use to soothe yourself by imagining your calmness.

5. You need to create your *Happy Book* or a *Piece of Happiness*. You can be the source of your happiness by filling yourself with happy words and get yourself all you need to feel happy above other people's influence on you.

#Method 2 – Learn to Confront your Emotions

Another method you need is to be able to confront your feelings. Do not run away from your emotions; rather, identify what your true emotions are. You need to pinpoint and identify your emotions. When your emotions are getting out of hand, you should look straight into them. Look into the source of your emotions. If your emotions are triggered by an upcoming examination, you can ask yourself what is getting you stressed out about the examination. You can name your emotions. By naming them, it will give you control over them. When you know what your emotions are, you have power over it. In learning to comfort your emotions, give yourself permission to work through your emotions. Take the following steps to confront your emotions.

1. Avoid ignoring your emotions. When you ignore them, they will always stay. They will bubble up and come back to resurface later. You should let yourself feel your emotions. Don't ruminate over them either. If you feel angry, you can either go out for a short walk or do yoga poses.

2. Think about what you can do to deal with the situation that warrants the emotions. Instead of thinking over soiled milk, why not just list out the challenges and identify the steps you can take to deal; with the situation accordingly. If there is anything you cannot work to deal with on your own, learn to let go of such.

3. Decide on how best you can move forward and make the next move. If you can resolve

the challenge, you should make the necessary move to deal with the issue. You can make a prior decision on how you want to deal with certain triggers. For example, you can make the decision that if someone insults you, rather than respond aggressively, you may decide to just walk out of the situation.

#Method 3 – Communicate with Confidence and Assertion

Be free to express your feelings without any restraint. When you learn to communicate assertively, you will exercise control over your emotions. You can say no to whatever it is that is making you feel uncomfortable. However, learn to do that tactfully. For example, if you are invited to a party, learn to decline if you observe that it will affect your emotions. Don't turn the host down blatantly, however, make him or she see the reason you cannot make it. You may say something like: "wow! Your invitation honors me. Thanks so much. But I do not like a large crowd, and I would love to pass this time. How about we create time to meet up for a coffee?" To practice confidence communication, do the following.

1. Learn to use the first-person singular pronoun "I" statements when you make your point so as not to blame others. If you are about saying anything, look critically at t, and if it seems to be judgmental or place blame on others, avoid it. To be practical, instead of telling someone that "Billy, you do not like me," say this, "I wasn't happy when you promised to call me back, but you didn't. What must have happened?"

2. Give room for others to share their opinions. When you give others the benefit of the doubt, you will permit them to share their opinion on a topic. When people are allowed to share their thoughts, you understand their emotions and their actions; hence, there will be a well-built relationship between you two. Also, you can easily calm yourself when you learn to listen to others.

3. Stay away from using judgmental language. When you keep blaming others, you will put yourself on the boulevard of frustration because people can never satisfy us; we need to identify the best way to deal with others, which is accepting them for who they are.

#Method 4 – Place yourself in Daily Calmness

You need to give yourself to routine exercise. Walking out from time to time will help you to relax and let go of the steam. You can give yourself to certain exercises, including swimming, walking, or running. All these will help you to calm yourself when you feel heightened by the triggers that surround you. Placing yourself in daily calmness will give you control over ant external influences over your emotions. It can be achieved through soothing, breathing techniques, and stretching exercises. You can take the following steps to calm yourself daily.

1. Always engage your senses in a new manner to soothe your body. Learn to focus on the beauty and calm appreciation of the world that surrounds you. You need to practice an attitude of gratitude as it will help you to calm down when you are about getting out of control. You may listen to soothing music, or pet a dog, or cat. You may even eat your favorite food and savor the taste.

2. Utilize self-touch that is soothing. We need affectionate touch for us to thrive. When you get yourself used to positive touch, it increases oxytocin, which is a hormone that helps to boost our mood and relieves stress. You will be bonded to others around you.

3. Give yourself to meditation. Meditation helps to clear the mind and relieves anxiety. At the same time, it helps to improve your ability to deal with stress.

#Method 5 – Make Move Toward Building Long-term peace

You need to make a move to let go of the past. You have to face the roots of your emotional turmoil so that you can move past it. Identify the source of your emotional turmoil, and you will be able to deal with it. Try to build a long-lasting relationship with others. It is important that you create an interest in conflict resolution. You cannot avoid disputes. However, you can make plans to settle them as they surface. To build long-term peace, you can do the following.

1. Learn to forgive others. You cannot afford to hold on to past grudges and expect your emotions to be balanced. They are two parallel lines that are not meant to meet. Others will always get on your bad side; hence, you need to make the decision ahead to tackle what they do to you. Accept others for who they are and learn to forgive and forget.

2. Practice self-reflection through the use of a journal. When you keep a record of your

emotions, it will be easier for you to monitor your emotions. You will have access to what triggers your emotions and be able to make the appropriate move toward dealing with them.

3. Start reframing your negative thoughts to positive thoughts. Negative thoughts will never make you have peace with others. They affect relationships and make it difficult to set up any long-lasting relationship with others. Learn to feed your mind with the right information. Look out for what is good about others, and not the evil they do to you. See the good about everyone, and relate with them based on their positive deeds.